L is for Lincoln

An Illinois Alphabet

Written by Kathy-jo Wargin and Illustrated by Gijsbert van Frankenhuyzen

Sleeping Bear Press
310 North Main Street
Chelsea, MI 48118
www.sleepingbearpress.com
1-800-487-2323

Sleeping Bear Press is an imprint of The Gale Group, Inc.
a division of Thomson Learning, Inc.

Printed and bound in China.

10 9 8 7 6 5 4 3

Library of Congress Cataloging-in-Publication Data on file.
ISBN: 1-58536-016-3

To Kathryn Louise from Illinois, who always used to visit our family in Minnesota when I was a little girl and tell me stories about the wonderful place where she lived. Your smile will always remain in my heart.

KATHY-JO

To Deborah Meyer, thanks for all your help, you were a great person to work with and we couldn't have done it without you.

GIJSBERT

Illinois is rich with artifacts. An ancient town called Cahokia, an important cultural center between 1050 and 1200 A.D., was once located near the confluence of the Mississippi and Missouri Rivers, in an area known as the American Bottom. Today, Cahokia is one of two U.S. sites listed on the United Nations World Heritage List and contains over 100 mounds, including Monks Mound, nearly 30 meters high with a base of 291 by 236 meters, and with four stepped terraces. When Cahokia was a thriving civilization, it produced arrowheads, axe heads, figurines, and other artifacts.

Illinois is also home to the Dickson Mounds, located in west-central Illinois. They contain copper and shell artifacts as well as stone pipes and pottery from the Mississippian culture that dates back at least 1,000 years.

A is for the Arrowheads hiding in the ground, special tools from long ago waiting to be found.

B is for Big Bluestem Grass
so green when it is new,
watch it grow so tall and swift
and turn to purple-blue.

Big Bluestem Grass is the official state prairie grass of Illinois. Long ago, when tallgrass prairie covered much of what is now Illinois, this type of prairie grass was abundant. Big Bluestem Grass can reach 3 to 10 feet in height, and as it grows, it turns from green to purple-blue.

B is also for Bluegill, the Illinois state fish, as well as Black Hawk, a renowned Native American Sauk chief and author from Illinois.

Bb

Now **C** is for Chicago
it's called the windy city,
and also for the cardinal
singing clear and pretty.

Chicago is the largest city in Illinois, and the third largest city in the United States. It is home to the tallest building in North America, the Sears Tower, which was built in 1973 and is 1,450 feet tall. It is also home to the largest building in America (excluding the Pentagon), which is called The Merchandise Mart. Chicago is also home to the Chicago River, which is the only river in the entire world that flows backward. The river was reversed in 1900 for sanitation purposes.

C is also for the Northern Cardinal, which lives here year-round and was selected in 1928 by a group of Illinois schoolchildren as the official state bird of Illinois. Males are a brilliant scarlet color, and females are soft brown with a hint of red. The Cardinal likes to eat insects, grains, and seeds, and can usually be found feeding on the ground or in low bushes.

The letter D is for Mr. Deere,
he knew farming was a toil
so he made a better plow
to slip through midwest soil.

John Deere was an inventor who revolutionized farming. When he moved to Grand DeTour, Illinois in 1836, he learned that cast-iron plows, which were used successfully in Eastern states, were not able to work through the thicker soils of the Midwest region. So Mr. Deere, along with the help of a friend, went on to invent Deere's Self-Polishing plow, a plow with a specially curved blade and parts polished so smooth that thick damp soil would not stick to them. This new piece of machinery made it possible for settlers to successfully farm in Illinois and other Midwest states.

The Eastern Ribbon Snake is endangered in the state of Illinois. It has a dark body with three yellow stripes and can reach a length of 40 inches when fully grown. This type of snake is active from March to late October, and likes to feed on amphibians such as toads, frogs, and salamanders. Eastern Ribbon Snakes can be found near the many rivers and streams of Illinois.

E e

Eastern Ribbon Snake starts with E striped with yellow do you see?

Sssssss. Ssssss. In the grass.

Ssssss. Ssssss. Moving fast!

Now **F** is for the Ferris Wheel
spinning through the air,
the very first one ever seen
was at a Chicago Fair.

The very first Ferris wheel ever seen
was at the World's Columbian
Exposition in Chicago, also known as
the Chicago World's Fair of 1893.
Built by George W. Ferris, this special
attraction was built with 36 cars that
could each hold up to 60 people, mak-
ing it possible to take more than 2,000
people for a spin at one time. It was
250 feet in diameter, 825 feet in
circumference, and weighed more
than 4,000 tons. This Ferris wheel was
gigantic compared to the amusement
park versions we know today.

F f

And the Greater Prairie Chicken starts with letter G,
a funny flying grassland bird
that calls out wild and free.

Oo-loo Oo-oo-loo!
Around the prairie
I see you!

The Greater Prairie Chicken, a brown bird with black pinfeathers along its neck, is an endangered species in Illinois, primarily due to the loss of its prairie habitat. Illinois is the farthest eastern location in which this type of prairie chicken can be found. It is a grassland bird that likes to fly by flapping and gliding, and has been known to fly at speeds of up to 50 miles per hour. That's almost as fast as we travel in our cars!

H h

H is for a library,
come and take a look!
It's named for Harold Washington;
would you like to find a book?

The Harold Washington Library Center, located in Chicago, is the world's largest public library with more than two million books on its shelves. It is named in honor of Harold Washington, Chicago's first African-American Mayor, elected to office in 1983. Mayor Harold Washington died in 1987, and is fondly remembered for his love of reading and regard for education.

Now the letter **I** stands for this:
The Illinois and Michigan Canal,
it opened up the wilderness
for every guy and gal.

I i

The Illinois and Michigan Canal opened in 1848. This 97-mile canal connects Lake Michigan with the Illinois River, ultimately linking the Atlantic Ocean and the Gulf of Mexico. It was one of the most important developments in history, allowing expansion and growth through Midwestern areas, primarily Illinois. It also played an enormous role in the growth and expansion of Chicago. Today, the region surrounding the canal is known as the Illinois and Michigan Canal National Heritage Corridor, a series of rare natural areas, state and local parks, filled with recreational and cultural opportunities.

J is for Jane Addams,
she was a pioneer.
Her spirit and her strength
helped many people here.

Jane Addams was an Illinois native born in Cedarville in 1860. She graduated from Rockford Female Seminary in 1881, and in 1889, with the help of a friend, went on to found Hull House, a large house in Chicago primarily dedicated to providing services to immigrants. In 1910, she was awarded the first honorary degree ever granted to a woman by Yale University. Among her other accomplishments, Addams founded the Women's International League for Peace and Freedom in 1919, and helped found the American Civil Liberties Union in 1920. In 1931, this pioneer was the first American woman to receive the Nobel Peace Prize. Ms. Addams died in 1935, and is buried in Cedarville.

Kk

In 1703, a group of French traders and their wives founded Kaskaskia at the confluence of the Mississippi and Kaskaskia Rivers. The residents later built a fort to protect them during the French and Indian wars from 1756 - 1763. This fort stood until 1766 when people from Kaskaskia destroyed it rather than ceding it to the British, who had recently gained control of the Illinois country. The British went ahead and built their own Fort Gage by converting a Jesuit mission into barracks for themselves. However, during the American Revolution, George Rogers Clark and his Kentucky "Long Knives" marched across southern Illinois and liberated the town on July 4, 1778. The people of Kaskaskia were overjoyed, and rang the parish bell which had been a gift to the Catholic church from King Louis XV. The bell then became known as "The Liberty Bell of the West." This special treasure bears an inscription stating, "For the church of Illinois—by the gift of the King."

And **K** is for Kaskaskia Bell,
it let freedom ring.
It was a very special gift
from a special king.

Abraham Lincoln was the 16th president of the United States of America. He moved to Macon City, Illinois in 1830, and lived in the state until he became president in 1861.

Considered by many people to be one of the greatest presidents who ever lived, because on January 1, 1863 he issued the Emancipation Proclamation which freed all people held as slaves within the United States. President Lincoln was assassinated on April 14, 1865 by John Wilkes Booth in Ford's Theatre in Washington D.C.

Now here we have a special man,
waiting in our book.
Do you wonder who it is? Come and take a look!

L is for Lincoln,
Illinois is his land.
He was president long ago
and known to be fair and grand.

M

M is for the Monarch
Flutter! Flutter! Through the sky.
It's so much fun to sit and watch
a pretty butterfly.

The Monarch butterfly is the official state insect of Illinois. This beautiful orange and black butterfly is found in Illinois from late spring to late fall. Most Monarch butterflies will winter in the mountains of central Mexico, some 2,000 miles away. In 1975 it was named the official state insect, one year after a third grade class from Decatur made the proposal.

M is also for the Mazon Creek Fossils, found in natural and man-made outcrops of Francis Creek Shale in the Grundy, Will, Kankakee, and Livingston counties. These fossils are important because they are exceptionally well-preserved and give us much information about life millions of years ago.

Nn

The first railroad locomotive to operate in Illinois was placed on a track called the Northern Cross in November of 1838. This section of track was only the second to be laid in the United States. It was called the Northern Cross possibly because the railroad line ran parallel to a trail known as the "Northern Crossing" of Illinois.

Now N is for the Northern Cross,
the first railroad in our state
to be drawn by locomotive,
it made transportation great!

Chug, chug, move along.
Chug, chug, fast and strong.

Mrs. O'Leary had a cow and O'Leary starts with O. Some people believe that her cow started the Chicago fire long ago.

The Great Chicago Fire was one of the worst fires in history. It destroyed the city of Chicago, raging from October 8 to 10 in the year of 1871. Although the fire devastated many families, homes, and buildings, Chicago quickly rebuilt itself. Many people believed the fire started from a spark when a cow kicked over a lantern in a barn. That cow belonged to Mrs. O'Leary, and despite the fact that Mrs. O'Leary was exonerated of charges, the legend continues to grow.

Pp

Illinois is nicknamed "The Prairie State" because it is renowned for its grassy, flat lands that once stretched from Indiana, west to Nebraska, and from Texas, north to the Canadian provinces. This tallgrass prairie was like a patchwork quilt of many different types of prairies. The prairies of Illinois vanished after the arrival of European settlers, although remnants can be found in some areas. At one time, Illinois was 22 million acres of prairie and 14 million acres of forest.

P is for the Prairie State
that's what people say.
It's great to live in Illinois
where pretty grasses sway.

Now Q is for Quincy
she was rough and ready.
The first fire engine in our state;
let's go boys, hold her steady!

Qq

Quincy No. 1, Rough and Ready was the name of the first fire engine in the state of Illinois. It was brought to the city of Quincy in 1839 and was manned by volunteers. The town of Quincy was also the first city to use a metropolitan alarm system back in 1901.

The lively, agile River Otter is an endangered species in Illinois. These animals love to linger and frolic along rivers, streams, creeks, lakes, and marshes. A full-grown otter can weigh between 10 and 33 pounds, and has a long body with short and powerful legs.

River Boats have long been a common sight in Illinois because of the many large rivers that weave through the state. In the 1830s, steamboats became more common on the waterways, opening up commerce and travel for the Midwest. Later, some river boats became floating palaces, running up and down the rivers for pleasure.

R r

R is for the River Boats
that float upon the water,
and also for an animal
called the River Otter.

S s

Springfield starts with letter **S**,
the capital of Illinois.
Here the rules and laws are made
for every girl and boy.

Music by Archibald Johnson

Springfield is the state capital of Illinois. But that wasn't always so. In 1809, when what we know as the state of Illinois was organized as the Illinois Territory, Kaskaskia was named its capital. In 1818, Illinois was named a state and Kaskaskia remained the capital until 1820, when it was moved to Vandalia. Soon thereafter, people from Illinois began to request the capital be moved to a more central location and in 1839 it was moved to Springfield.

Although there have been three locations, there have actually been six different capitol buildings. The first was built in Kaskaskia, and three different buildings were used in Vandalia. The fifth building, which was built in Springfield in 1853, was used until the present capitol, on which construction was started in 1868, was completed 20 years later.

T is for the Tully Monster—
it was an animal in motion,
swimming through the water
when our state was just an ocean.

Splish Splash. Gone in a flash!

The Tully Monster is the state fossil of Illinois. More than 300 million years ago when most of Illinois was an ocean, this creature was a soft-bodied animal that swam freely in the water. Today, we find it in outlines and flat forms created in ironstone, mostly in places like the Mazon Creek deposits located in Will and Grundy counties. Some scientists believe that it may be related to snails or other mollusks. This fossil was discovered by Mr. Francis Tully in 1958.

Tt

U is for Ulysses Grant
a hero from long ago.
He was a general in the war
and our president, did you know?

Ulysses S. Grant was the 18th president of the United States of America. Prior to his presidency, he was a Union General during the Civil War and a great military hero. In 1860 he moved his family to Galena, Illinois, and in 1861 he was appointed Colonel of the 21st Illinois Regiment of Infantry. Later that year, Grant was promoted to Brigadier General and assigned to the District of Southeast Missouri in Cairo, Illinois. General Grant won many battles and was eventually promoted to General of the Army. The most famous battle ended when Grant forced General Lee to surrender to him at Appomattox Court House on April 9, 1865.

He was elected president immediately after the war, serving from 1869 to 1877.

V

Violet starts with the letter V,
a dainty purple flower
peeking through the grass so green
in a bright sunshower!

The violet has been the official state flower of Illinois since 1908. This native wildflower grows in sunlight or shade. The violet actually produces two types of flowers: a large showy flower in the spring, and then later in the season, small flowers on short stems appear close to the ground. The small bud-like flowers near the ground will produce most of the violet seeds.

The White Oak is the official state tree of Illinois. Its thick heavy branches make it a very good shade tree, and it commonly grows to heights of 100 feet or more. The white oak will begin to produce acorns when it is approximately 20 years old. In 1907, Illinois school-children selected the native oak as the official state tree. It wasn't until 1973 that a special poll changed the designation from native oak to white oak.

W also stands for William Wrigley Jr., a businessman who made chewing gum a household favorite, as well as Oprah Winfrey, talk-show host and actress.

W

White Oak starts with W,
a tall and sturdy tree.
Acorns falling to the ground,
some for you and some for me.

X is for the pattern
the Illinois Central makes,
when it crosses with great speed
it rumbles and it shakes.

Toot toot!

The Illinois Central Railroad was chartered in 1851, the first railroad in the country to make use of a federal land grant. The railroad was completed in 1856, and went from Cairo to Galena and Chicago. In 1861, the Central's regular service was interrupted so the railroad could move troops and supplies through Cairo. Eventually, the ICR linked to many other railroads, providing a nucleus for greater transportation opportunities throughout the country.

STOP

RAIL ROAD CROSSING

2 TRACKS

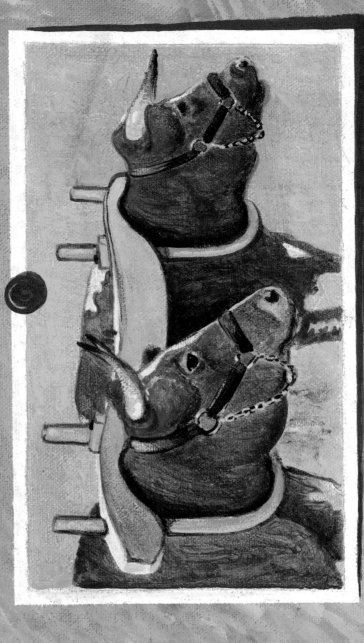

Y

Y

The yellow fields of Illinois tell us that agriculture is a primary industry here. More than 28 million acres, which is nearly 80 percent of the state's total land area, is covered by farms. Cold dry winters and warm humid summers help provide good farming conditions, as does the fertile flat land left behind by glaciers millions of years ago.

Illinois ranks third in the nation for total "prime farm" acreage, which means the farmland is well suited for providing an environmentally sound base for livestock and crops. Illinois is well-known for corn and soybeans, swine, sorghum, hay, wheat, oats, sheep, buckwheat, and even horseradish.

Yellow fields of wheat and corn
start with letter Y,
rolling in the summer breeze
growing oh so high!

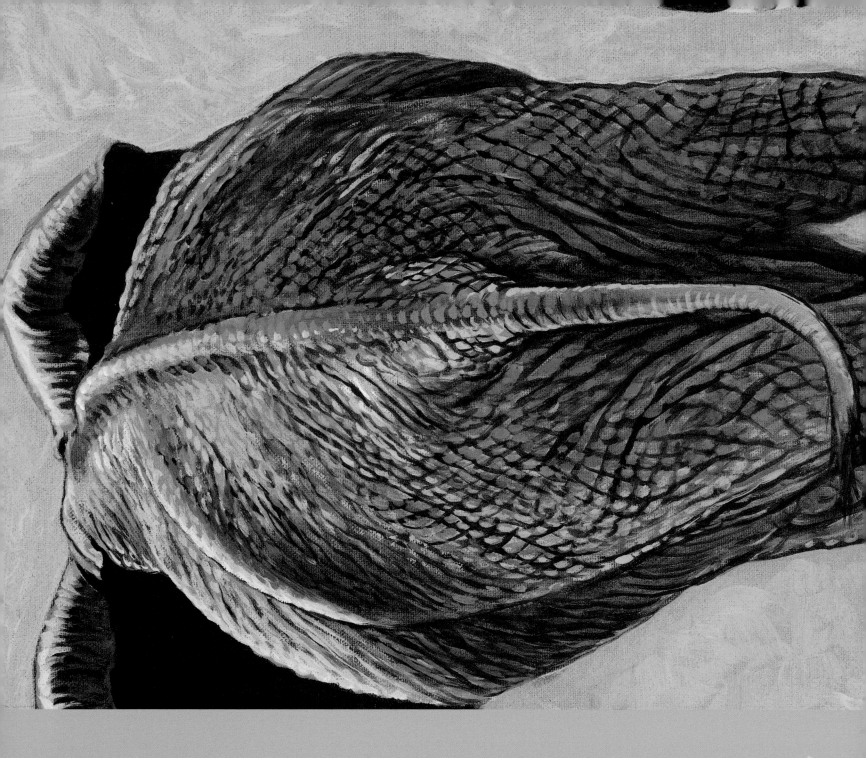

In 1868, two swans from New York's Central Park were given to the newly established Lincoln Park Zoo. Today, Lincoln Park Zoo is the nation's oldest zoo, and one of the most visited zoos in the country. As well, it is one of the last "free" zoos remaining, which means there is no charge for admittance.

Z is for the Lincoln Park Zoo,
the oldest zoo in the USA!
It's fun to watch the animals
eat and drink and play.

Now we've said the ABCs
it's fun as fun can be
and we've discovered Illinois
from the letters A to Z!

Lincoln Park Zoo

A Prairie Full of Facts

1. Starved Rock State Park in 1911.

2. It is Carlyle Lake, located in the southern portion of the state, and it covers 26,000 acres.

3. In 1955.

4. In 1833.

5. Cracker Jacks in 1893, and Hostess Twinkies in 1930.

6. Corn, swine, soybeans, cattle, wheat, sorghum, hay, and sheep are a few.

7. Peoria.

8. The Sears Tower, in Chicago.

9. The Staley Bears, organized in Decatur in 1920.

10. In Dixon, Illinois.

11. The Illinois River.

12. In 1871.

13. Soldier Field, United Center, Wrigley Field, and Comiskey Park.

14. Metropolis, Illinois, was officially declared the Hometown of Superman by the Illinois House in 1972.

15. The Kaskaskia, Cahokia, Peoria, Tamaroa, and Michigamea people.

16. Lac du Illinois, because of its proximity to the people who inhabited the region and were known as the Illini.

---

1. Which park became the first state park in Illinois?

2. Do you know the name of the state's largest inland water system?

3. When did O'Hare Airport open for operation?

4. When was Chicago incorporated as a town?

5. What tasty confections were first produced in Illinois?

6. What types of agricultural goods come from Illinois?

7. What is the oldest community in Illinois?

8. What is the tallest building on the North American continent?

9. When the Chicago Bears were first organized, what were they called?

10. Where did former President Ronald Regan live as a boy?

11. What is the largest river in the state?

12. What year was the Great Chicago Fire?

13. Can you name four major sports stadiums located in Chicago?

14. What Illinois city declares it is the hometown of a superhero?

15. What people comprised the Illini Confederation?

16. When the French arrived upon what we now know as Lake Michigan, what did they call it?